21ST
Century
Skills Library

COOL MILITARY CAREERS

PARARESCUE

NANCY ROBINSON

CHERRY LAKE
Publishing

Published in the United States of America by
Cherry Lake Publishing, Ann Arbor, Michigan
www.cherrylakepublishing.com

Content Adviser
Cynthia Watson, PhD, author of *U.S. National Security*

Credits
Cover and pages 1, 4, 6, 15, 20, and 29, U.S. Air Force photo by Master Sgt.
Russell E Cooley IV/Released; page 9, U.S. Air Force photo by Staff Sgt. Jason
Robertson/Released; pages 10 and 16, U.S. Air Force photo by Master Sgt. Shane A.
Cuomo/Released; pages 12 and 26, U.S. Air Force photo by Staff Sgt. Joseph L.
Swafford Jr./Released; page 13, DoD photo by Staff Sgt. James L. Harper Jr., U.S.
Air Force/Released; page 18, U.S. Air Force photo by Staff Sgt. Manuel J. Martinez/
Released; page 22, U.S. Air Force photo by Airman 1st Class Lausanne Morgan/
Released; page 23, U.S. Air Force photo by Staff Sgt. Heather M. Norris/Released;
page 25, U.S. Air Force photo by Staff Sgt. Chris Willis/Released

Library of Congress Cataloging-in-Publication Data
Masters, Nancy Robinson.
  Pararescue jumper/by Nancy Robinson Masters.
      p. cm.—(Cool military careers) (21st century skills library)
  Includes bibliographical references and index.
  Audience: Grades 2–6.
  ISBN 978-1-61080-451-6 (lib. bdg.) — ISBN 978-1-61080-538-4 (e-book) —
ISBN 978-1-61080-625-1 (pbk.)
  1. United States. Air Force—Parachute troops—Juvenile literature. 2. United
States. Air Force—Search and rescue operations—Juvenile literature. 3. United
States. Air Force—Vocational guidance—Juvenile literature. 4. Special forces
(Military science)—United States—Juvenile literature. I. Title.
  UG633.M3197 2012
  356'.1664—dc23   2012010225

Cherry Lake Publishing would like to acknowledge
the work of The Partnership for 21st Century Skills.
Please visit *www.21stcenturyskills.org* for more information.

Printed in the United States of America
Corporate Graphics Inc.
July 2012
CLFA11

TABLE OF CONTENTS

CHAPTER ONE
**WHAT IS A PARARESCUE
JUMPER?** 4

CHAPTER TWO
**BECOMING A PARARESCUE
JUMPER** 10

CHAPTER THREE
**PLANNING, PRACTICING, AND
PERFORMING RESCUES** 20

CHAPTER FOUR
JUMPING INTO THE FUTURE . . . 26

GLOSSARY .30
FOR MORE INFORMATION 31
INDEX 32
ABOUT THE AUTHOR 32

CHAPTER ONE

WHAT IS A PARARESCUE JUMPER?

"Look up, Dad!"

Brien was the first in his family to spot the airplane circling above the 10,000-foot-long (3,048-meter) runway at

Parachutes allow rescue jumpers to drop in wherever they are needed.

Dyess Air Force Base in Texas. An empty plastic wading pool like the one in which he bathed his dog sat in the middle of the huge runway. Thousands of air show spectators watched as three **parachutes** suddenly popped open high above the crowd. The air show announcer's voice asked, "Ladies and gentlemen, which of these three men will be the first to land on his feet inside the wading pool?"

"I pick the one with the blue streamers," Brien said.

"I pick the one with the red streamers," his dad replied.

The crowd began to cheer as each of the men carefully maneuvered his parachute toward the wading pool target.

"You were both wrong," said Brien's mom. "The man with the parachute flying the flag of the United States of America landed first!"

The announcer's voice brought even more cheers and applause from Brien and the other spectators.

"Ladies and gentlemen, you've just seen a demonstration of the amazing skills used to save lives by our United States pararescue jumpers!"

■ ■ ■

Pararescue jumpers (PJs) serve in the United States Air Force. They are part of the Air Force Special Operations Command. This special operations unit is headquartered at Hurlburt Field in Florida. The mission of this unit is to save lives and recover equipment in areas of danger, such as combat zones, or in areas that are difficult to reach because of the **terrain** or other obstacles.

Finding ways to rescue fellow service members and essential equipment has always been a goal of U.S. military leaders. PJs were first used to carry out these types of missions during

Pararescue jumpers rely on their teammates to help them complete missions successfully.

World War II (1939–1945). Since then, specially trained PJs have saved thousands of lives all over the world, including Iraq and Afghanistan, where conflicts were ongoing in the early 2000s.

LIFE & CAREER SKILLS

Part of the oath taken by pararescue jumpers says, "I will be prepared at all times to perform my assigned duties quickly and efficiently. . . . These things I do, that others may live." Making this promise is a serious personal commitment that you should consider carefully when thinking about a career as a pararescue jumper. For example, pararescue combat rescue officers are responsible for planning and managing rescue operations that may involve hundreds of people. They must have superb leadership abilities and be prepared to teach others survival, evasion, resistance, and escape skills.

Pararescue jumpers work together as part of a team on a wide variety of missions. For example, pararescue jumpers may parachute from aircraft into a remote area to provide emergency medical treatment to someone who is injured. The PJs would also be responsible for getting the injured person to safety. A pararescue jumper may be assigned to recover a computer containing secret information from an airplane that has been shot down in enemy territory. In any situation, the PJ depends on other team members such as pilots, mechanics, and mission planners to get the job done.

Pararescue jumpers in the air force work in partnership with the U.S. Army, Navy, Marines, and Coast Guard. They work most often with the Navy's Sea, Air, and Land teams (SEALs). They also support the National Aeronautics and Space Administration (NASA) and work with **civilian** emergency agencies during natural disasters such as earthquakes, floods, hurricanes, and wildfires.

Pararescue jumpers are called in to handle a variety of dangerous situations.

CHAPTER TWO
BECOMING A PARARESCUE JUMPER

A ll members of the Air Force, Army, Navy, Marines, and Coast Guard chose to join the armed forces.

Pararescue jumpers work hard to help keep their country safe.

Choosing to join the Air Force is the first step to becoming a pararescue jumper. An Air Force **recruiter** can provide all of the application information and paperwork you need to enlist if you are not a college graduate. You can also join through the Reserve Officers' Training Corps program (ROTC) offered through some colleges and universities as part of a college degree program.

Think carefully about why you want to be a pararescue jumper. If the challenges of parachuting, scuba diving, and an active, fast-paced life appeal to you, this might be a career worth pursuing. If you're in it for the glory or a big paycheck, you're making the wrong choice. Also, make sure your family understands why you want to become a PJ, because it's important that they support your decision.

Before you enlist with a recruiter or join the ROTC, learn all you can about salaries, benefits, and career opportunities that you'll receive as an airman or officer in the Air Force. For example, tuition assistance is an education benefit that pays tuition and fees for college courses taken by active-duty personnel. This helps you earn a college degree while you're in the Air Force.

You also need to know what challenges you will face and what career opportunities will be available to you *after* you complete your military career. If you decide to join, you'll be required to sign a contract. The contract explains the rules, rights, and responsibilities you agree to accept when you join.

All members of the air force go through basic training, sometimes called boot camp, at Lackland Air Force Base in San Antonio, Texas, to learn discipline and teamwork. Basic training prepares you mentally and physically to be a soldier. After completing basic training, you may apply for pararescue training if you are a male citizen of the United States with a high school diploma. Women cannot serve as PJs. It is one of the few U.S. military careers not available to females.

Pararescue jumpers must be able to work alone in remote areas.

Pararescue jumpers cannot be afraid of heights.

You must also pass the Armed Services Vocational Aptitude Battery (ASVAB). The ASVAB tests you on basic skills such as general science, word and mathematics knowledge, automotive maintenance and repair, and electronics. All PJ applicants must also pass a background check for a **security clearance** to ensure that you are a trustworthy person and loyal to the United States of America.

If you meet these requirements, you must then pass a test of your physical abilities before you are eligible for selection. Can you

- swim 20 meters (66 feet) underwater on one breath?
- swim 500 meters (1,640 feet) in 16 minutes or less?
- run 1.5 miles (2.4 kilometers) in under 10½ minutes?
- do eight chin-ups in a minute or less?
- do 50 sit-ups in two minutes or less?
- do 50 push-ups in two minutes or less?

You must be able to do all of these during the three-hour physical abilities test to prove you are ready for pararescue jumper training.

Competition to become a pararescue jumper is fierce. If you are selected as a pararescue jumper trainee, you will begin a series of training courses called the pipeline. The pararescue jumper pipeline involves some of the most intense training of any military specialty. Roughly 70 to 80 percent of the trainees fail to make it through the course. It takes about two years to complete all of the courses. The courses push trainees to their

All pararescue jumpers must be very strong swimmers.

physical and mental limits. Staying calm and in control is a must. During the training, you won't see much of your family or friends. You'll spend most of your time with your teammates building teamwork skills.

Courses are conducted at different locations and include:

- Pararescue/Combat Control, 9 weeks: intense swimming, running, and weight training
- U.S. Army Airborne School, 3 weeks: basic parachuting skills

Training exercises help pararescuemen learn how to deal with any situation they might encounter in the field.

LIFE & CAREER SKILLS

Pararescue jumpers are among the most highly trained emergency medical technicians (EMTs) in the U.S. military. They perform "dirt medicine," treating everything from minor injuries to life-or-death combat injuries. After they complete their Air Force careers, pararescue personnel usually have many opportunities to use their EMT skills in a civilian career. EMTs can work in a variety of settings, including ambulances, factories, fire departments, and hospitals.

- U.S. Air Force Combat Diver Course, 6 weeks: underwater diving skills
- U.S. Air Force Basic Survival School, 2½ weeks: learning to survive on your own with limited resources in dangerous or remote locations
- U.S. Army Military Freefall Parachutist School, 5 weeks: advanced parachuting skills
- Paramedic, 22 weeks: emergency medical technician training

One of a PJ's most important pieces of equipment is his parachute. The four main parts of a parachute are the **canopy**, the container, the lines, and the risers. The canopy is the parachute itself, the part that opens up above the jumper. The container is the backpack that holds the parachute. The lines run from the parachute to the container through the risers, a pair of thick straps.

PJs use different parachute designs depending on the kind of mission they're assigned to. The MC1 parachute design is

Pararescue jumpers must be extremely familiar with the different parts of their parachutes.

used most often for a planned jump into a small target area. The parachute canopy is dome shaped and opens fast and with a jolt! It allows the PJ to descend straight down at 10 to 25 feet (3.0 to 7.6 m) per second depending on the weight of the jumper. The chute of an MC1 is made of a special kind of nylon material and weighs about 29 pounds (13.2 kilograms) when it is packed. The canopy opens to a diameter of about 24 feet (7.3 m). An MC1 parachute must be opened at least 500 feet (152 m) above the ground.

A ram air canopy is a newer parachute design used by pararescue jumpers who **free fall** from high altitudes before opening their parachutes. The ram air canopy is also made of nylon but is rectangular in shape. A ram air canopy gives the PJ more control than a traditional dome-shaped canopy.

Safely managing a parachute after landing is as important as controlling it in the air. A pararescue jumper can be injured or killed if he fails to follow the proper procedures for releasing from the parachute harness and container once he lands.

When a trainee successfully completes his years of training, he is awarded a maroon beret with the pararescue flash emblem, certifying him as a U.S. Air Force PJ. His training and expert equipment-handling skills have prepared him to do his dangerous job anywhere in the world.

CHAPTER THREE
PLANNING, PRACTICING, AND PERFORMING RESCUES

"Quality first."

That's the motto pararescue jumpers learn during their first week of training. PJs spend more time planning and

Careful planning helps prevent mistakes during dangerous or difficult missions.

practicing than performing actual rescues. They plan how they will drop into an area and how to deal with any kind of search-and-rescue mission once they're on the ground. The four most essential skills they practice are called SERE:

- **S**urvival
- **E**vasion, or avoiding the enemy
- **R**esistance, or fighting to avoid capture
- **E**scape

During the wars in Iraq and Afghanistan in the early 2000s, PJs put SERE skills to use almost every day. The rescue squadron based at Camp Bastion, Afghanistan, included pararescue jumpers, flight crews, maintenance workers, and supply personnel. When the rescue squadron received a report of a downed U.S. helicopter, military commanders immediately began planning a pararescue mission. Two PJs parachuted into an area that vehicles could not reach. Using their search skills and equipment, they found the downed aircrew while evading enemy attack.

One PJ gave emergency medical care to one of the wounded aircrew members, while the other PJ guarded the area until rescue helicopters arrived. After the aircrew members were safely aboard the rescue helicopter, another rescue helicopter picked up the PJs. The success of the mission was due to the SERE skills that the pararescue team had practiced and used. To date, pararescue jumpers have been credited with saving more than 1,000 lives in Iraq and Afghanistan.

Pararescue jumpers also carry out missions in water. Because they train to be excellent swimmers, PJs can rescue aircrews whose planes are downed over seas, lakes, or rivers.

Not all rescue missions occur in war zones. Military pararescue jumpers are often called upon to use their rescue skills when there is a natural disaster somewhere in the world. PJs are credited with helping save more than 4,000 lives after Hurricane Katrina hit the U.S. Gulf Coast in 2005.

Pararescue jumpers can quickly evacuate injured people from danergous areas.

Pararescue jumpers must be prepared to leave on a mission with little notice.

If you're interested in a career as a military PJ, you might be curious to know how much you can expect to earn. In addition to their regular Air Force salary, which is based on **rank** and time served in the military, pararescue jumpers may also receive bonus pay. The bonus pay amount is currently less than $1,000 a month. PJs are eligible for retirement after 20 years of military service.

LEARNING & INNOVATION SKILLS

A pararescue jumper is far more than a skilled parachutist. He can parachute into areas wearing a full suit of scuba-diving equipment, allowing him to provide rescue and recovery support for water rescues. He is an expert with maps and a compass, and he can travel overland in any hostile environment, include mountains and Arctic regions. Most PJs are required to be on alert status and ready to jump into action 24 hours a day.

Pararescue jumpers are able to complete remarkable maneuvers in almost any environment.

CHAPTER FOUR
JUMPING INTO THE FUTURE

There are roughly 400 pararescue jumpers serving in the U.S. military today. Each of them is ready to take his skills and jump into the future, saving lives and protecting the United States at home and abroad. New technology such as the

Ram air parachutes help pararescue jumpers make accurate landings.

Global Positioning System (GPS) is making it possible to find downed aircraft and aircrews more quickly. Better emergency medical treatment methods are helping to save more lives. Advanced parachute designs help jumpers maneuver more safely and land more accurately in dangerous areas.

The use of **drones**, or unmanned aerial vehicles, will bring even more changes for pararescue jumpers in the future. Computer-operated drones are already being used in place of manned aircraft in many combat operations. U.S. military planners believe drones will reduce the number of people needed to fly dangerous missions in the future.

Although drones may help reduce the number of people downed or injured in combat, there will still be a need for military pararescue jumpers. The most important qualifications to be a pararescue jumper today will not change in the future. If you choose to be a PJ, you'll still need to

- prepare for physical and mental challenges;
- care about others;
- have a positive attitude;
- think quickly and act carefully;
- follow directions correctly;
- be physically fit;
- work well as part of a team;
- enjoy being outdoors; and
- be dedicated and disciplined.

Remember, keeping your cool will always be one of the most important parts of a cool career as a pararescue jumper.

21ˢᵀ CENTURY CONTENT

In 2011, Technical Sergeant Kristopher Burridge had been a PJ jumper for 17 years. Senior Airman Jackson Rogers had just started his career as a PJ. Captain John Mosier was a rescue helicopter pilot. That year, these three Americans were awarded the French National Defense Medal for their heroic actions to save a downed French helicopter crew during a dangerous mission in Afghanistan. The rescue on the ground took only nine minutes, but getting a medal from the French government was not on their minds that night. The three airmen said they were just doing their job. "Getting guys out of tough spots—that's what it's all about," said Captain Mosier.

Do you have what it takes to serve as a pararescue jumper?

GLOSSARY

canopy (KAN-uh-pee) the portion of a parachute that opens and slows the fall of the jumper

civilian (suh-VIL-yuhn) not part of the armed forces

drones (DROHNZ) unmanned aerial vehicles that are controlled remotely

free fall (FREE FAWL) the part of a parachute jump before the parachute opens

Global Positioning System (GLOH-buhl puh-ZISH-uhn-ing SIS-tuhm) a space-based satellite navigation system that provides location and time information anywhere on Earth

parachutes (PAR-uh-shoots) large pieces of fabric attached to thin ropes that spread out in the air to slow the fall of whatever is attached to them

rank (RANGK) official job level or position

recruiter (ri-KROO-tur) a military employee in charge of signing up new members and providing information to people who are interested in joining the military

security clearance (si-KYOOR-i-tee KLEER-uhns) the status of a person in regard to how much access to secret information they are allowed

terrain (tuh-RAYN) the surface features of an area of land

FOR MORE INFORMATION

BOOKS

Hamilton, John. *Unmanned Aerial Vehicles*. Minneapolis, MN: ABDO, 2012.

Porterfield, Jason. *USAF Special Tactics Teams*. New York: Rosen Publishing, 2008.

Sandler, Michael. *Pararescuemen in Action*. New York: Bearport Publishing, 2008.

WEB SITES

HowStuffWorks—How Skydiving Works
http://adventure.howstuffworks.com/skydiving2.htm
Find out more about parachutes and how they work.

U.S. Air Force
www.airforce.com
Check out this site to learn more about careers, benefits, and life in the U.S. Air Force, and to view videos of parachutists, jets, and spacecraft in high-flying action.

USAF Pararescue—Savings Lives at 26,000 Feet
www.pararescue.com/unitinfo.aspx?id=482
A great site to read about pararescue training and the history and responsibilities of military pararescue, and to read a fascinating interview with a PJ.

INDEX

Afghanistan, 7, 21, 28

Air Force, 5, 8, 10–11

Air Force Special Operations Command, 5

ASVAB (Armed Services Vocational Aptitude Battery) test, 14

basic training, 12

benefits, 11, 24

Camp Bastion, 21

canopy, 18, 19

contracts, 11

drones, 27

education, 11

EMTs (emergency medical technicians), 17

enlistment, 10–11

free fall, 19

Iraq, 7, 21

MC1 parachutes, 18–19

missions, 5–8, 18, 20–22, 27, 28

motto, 20

natural disasters, 8, 22

Navy SEALs (Sea, Air, and Land teams), 8

parachutes, 5, 16, 17, 18–19, 21, 27

physical abilities, 12, 14, 16, 27

planning, 7, 20–21

ram air canopy, 19

recruiters, 11

retirement, 24

ROTC (Reserve Officers' Training Corps), 11

salary, 11, 24

security clearance, 14

SERE (Survival, Evasion, Resistance, Escape) skills, 21

skills, 7, 14, 16, 17, 19, 21

swimming, 14, 16, 22, 24

team members, 7, 8, 16, 21, 27

terrain, 6, 21, 24

tests, 14

training, 12, 14, 16–17, 19, 20, 22

women, 12

World War II, 7

ABOUT THE AUTHOR

Nancy Robinson Masters is a civilian pilot and author of more than 40 books. She has never jumped out of an airplane. She lives in the Elmdale Community near Abilene, Texas, at a private airport with her husband, veteran aviator Bill Masters. She and her husband have both received the Distinguished Citizen of the Year Award from the United States Air Force. This award is in recognition of their support of the U.S. military.